D1389258

THE OFFICIAL
HIBERNIAN
FOOTBALL CLUB ANNUAL **2011**

Written by David Forsyth

Designed by Brian Thomson

A Grange Publication

© 2010. Published by Grange Communications Ltd., Edinburgh under licence from Hibernian Football Club.

Printed in the EU.

Photography © SNSPix.

ISBN: 978-1-907104-65-7

£7.99

CONTENTS

CHAIRMAN'S
· ·
WELCOME

Each season brings its own highs and lows, and the season just past was no exception.

A magnificent first two-thirds of the season, which included a 12-match unbeaten run, saw Hibernian threatening Rangers and Celtic at the top of the league, and attract plaudits for an expansive and entertaining style of play.

However, a dip in form which included a disappointing Scottish Cup exit to Ross County threatened to undo all of the good work put in by the manager, coaches and players earlier in the season until, with a final high on the rollercoaster, the team rose to the pressure on the last match of the season to snatch Europa League football.

During the season Scottish football came in for some heavy criticism, much of it undeserved in my opinion. Despite a freakishly severe winter, the SPL continued to provide excitement right up until the final day, with last season's interest in the three-way battle for Europe going right down to the wire. That said, those of us involved in running the professional game must always be open to new ideas and change, and debate around the future of the sport we love is to be welcomed.

Everyone at the Club is delighted that the redevelopment of Easter Road is complete with the new East Stand, with our stadium now unquestionably the finest in Scotland outside of Glasgow. It is a further demonstration that the strategy long pursued by your Board, of incremental progress based on a self-sufficient and sustainable business, continues to be the progressive model now being followed by more and more Clubs.

Enjoy the Annual, and support the team!

season
review
2009/10

PRE-SEASON:

The season began with a full programme of friendlies, both in Scotland against lower league opposition and in the north of England, where opponents included English Premiership sides Blackburn Rovers and Bolton Wanderers.

AUGUST:

The competitive matches kicked off on August 15th, when St Mirren visited Easter Road. An exciting match was decided late in the game when a Benji diving header secured a 2-1 win. A trip to Falkirk saw John Hughes return to his former Club for the first time as Hibs manager, and a 3-1 win over the Bairns with goals from Bamba and Riordan (2) ensured the grin stayed in place. Brechin City were the visitors in the League Cup in a game when goals from Riordan, own goal and Hanlon saw a comfortable progression. The month was seen out when Celtic visited Easter Road, the Parkhead men fortunate to emerge 1-0 victors in a hard-fought encounter.

SEPTEMBER:

A disappointing visit to Hamilton at the start of the month saw Hibs lose 2-0 in a poor performance, but much better was to follow. St Johnstone were beaten 3-0 next up at Easter Road, with goals from Stokes (2) and Riordan. The match was more even than the score suggested, and when the Perth men returned a few days later on League Cup business a Stokes' strikes was consolation in a 3-1 defeat. The league itself was proving a much happier hunting ground, and a potentially tricky away trip to Motherwell was safely navigated with a thrilling 3-1 win courtesy of goals from Nish, Riordan and Zemmama.

OCTOBER:

Dundee United were the visitors at the start of October, and a goal by Zemmama was cancelled out in the second-half in an exciting 1-1 draw between two teams destined to spend the season jostling for a Europa League spot. Kilmarnock were next at Easter Road, and a Benji penalty was enough to divide the teams. A visit to Rangers at Ibrox was next, and a brilliant goal by Stokes earned a point in a magnificent match, before the month ended with a strong performance in a 2-0 win against Aberdeen with Nish and Miller on the scoresheet.

NOVEMBER:

The first derby of the season kicked November off, with the game at Tynecastle ending in a hard-fought 0-0 draw. Another away trip followed, to Paisley, where a Riordan strike saw Hibs gain a point on the road. Riordan was again on target – twice – as Hibs saw Falkirk off by a 2-0 margin at Easter Road to keep their unbeaten league run going.

DECEMBER:

The festive month saw Hibs in festive mood, flying high in the league and strongly tipped for a high finish. That confidence seemed well-placed as Motherwell were beaten 2-0 with Stokes scoring both. The Irish striker was again on target as the club travelled to Kilmarnock to earn another draw away from home, and the good form on the road continued at Pittodrie as goals from hot-shot Stokes secured all three points in a 2-0 win. The visit of Rangers to Easter Road was much anticipated, with the two form teams in the country tussling, but despite a quick stroke from Stokes the visitors were in dominant mood and Hibs lost out by the disappointing margin of 4-1. The end of the year had brought an end to a long unbeaten run, with Hibs playing 12 without defeat.

JANUARY:

The New Year began strongly, with Hearts the visitors as the derby again finished honours-even, with Stokes earning a point in a 1-1 draw. History was made when Junior side Irvine Meadow came to visit on Scottish Cup business, the Ayrshire side performing well but eventually losing 3-0 through goals by Riordan, Zemmama and Hanlon. Another loss, this time away to Dundee United by a single goal, was followed by a run of three straight wins. First, Hamilton were crushed 5-1 at Easter Road with Nish, Stokes(2) and Riordan (2) all bulging the net. A superb late goal at Parkhead then saw Hibs beat Celtic 2-1 in Glasgow, Galbraith netting the winner after an earlier Stokes' strike. Liam Miller was again on the scoresheet as St Mirren were beaten 2-1 at Easter Road, along with an own goal.

FEBRUARY:

Montrose came to Easter Road in the Scottish Cup 5th Round, only to suffer a 5-1 defeat with goals by Nish (2), Riordan, Benji and Gow. A stirring second-half fightback saw Hibs show great spirit to snatch a 2-2 draw at Easter Road against Aberdeen after being two goals behind, with Stokes and Benji the scorers. A trip to face Rangers ended with a similar margin of defeat as the earlier match between the two, with a 3-0 reverse, but worse was to follow when a trip to Perth to face St Johnstone provided a low point of the season with a crushing 5-1 defeat suffered, a Stokes' strike providing scant consolation. A narrow away loss to Motherwell by 1-0 followed, with Hibs forced to play much of the game with 10 men after Miller was unfortunate to be red-carded, and the month ended with a 1-1 draw with St Johnstone at Easter Road, with that man Stokes again on target.

MARCH:

A busy month kicked off in more encouraging style, with a 1-0 win at Easter Road against Kilmarnock courtesy of a storming Riordan free kick. A late goal earned First Division Ross County a draw in the Quarter-Final of the Scottish Cup at Easter Road, and a replay in Dingwall. An away derby at Tynecastle ended in a 2-1 defeat, with Riordan again scoring against our old rivals, and then a match which provided the low-point of the season when Hibernian went out of the cup to an injury time winner losing 2-1 to Ross County

APRIL:

The final two matches before the split saw Celtic again secure a narrow 1-0 win at Easter Road, before a visit to Hamilton saw another poor defeat, this time by 4-1 with a Nish goal providing the only bright spot for Hibs fans. The team went into the final round of matches again the

MAY:

Hearts came to Easter Road seeking to close the gap, and left with the points after securing a 2-1 win despite Hibs taking the lead through a Stokes' penalty. Next up came the most talked about match of the season, as Hibs visited Motherwell. The men

DUTCH COURAGE

EDWIN de GRAAF

The pre-season signing last summer of Dutch star Edwin de Graaf saw a genuine leader come to Hibernian.

The 30-year-old midfield powerhouse has captained sides in the Netherlands' top league, including his last club NAC Breda.

His leadership qualities, his experience and his physical strength all helped make up the mind of manager John Hughes to sign the Dutchman – but most of all it was his football ability.

The gaffer said: "He is a real gem, and brings with him a wealth of experience gained at a high level. He has played regularly throughout his career in the Eredivisie and also in the UEFA Cup.

Edwin de Graaf

Born: 30th April 1980 in The Hague

Height: 6ft 1in

Position: Midfielder

Previous Clubs: RBC Roosendaal, Feyenoord, ADO Den Haag, NAC Breda

International Caps: 5 times capped at B team level for Netherlands

"He is powerful, a real box-to-box player and he scores goals as well. He is a real asset for the team."

For his part, De Graaf was sold on moving to Edinburgh after seeing around the city, the training centre and Easter Road -- and after talking to old team-mate and former Rangers striker Michael Mols.

He said: "It is great to be a part of a Club with such a great set-up and such a great history, and I have been told by Dutch players who have been in Scotland that the people are friendly and passionate about the game. I am happy to be here."

HIBS KIDS
JOIN TODAY
0844
844
1875

"LAST MINUTE" LAWRIE REILLY

· ·

HIBERNIAN LEGEND

Lawrie Reilly

Born: October 28th 1928 in Edinburgh

Position: Striker

International Caps: 38 (Hibernian's most capped player)

Additional Information:

- Club goal scoring record holder
- Played for Hibernian in inaugural European Cup
- Played for the Club on tour in Brazil, Canada, USA
- Played in record-breaking derby in January 1950, when a huge crowd of 65,860 was in attendance at Easter Road
- In his 253 league appearances for the club Reilly scored 185 goals and 47 others in cup-ties

The term "legend" is often bandied about too easily. But not when it is applied to former Hibernian star Lawrie Reilly.

A member of the all-conquering "Famous Five" forward line that terrorised defences around the world — and still regarded by many as the greatest ever British forward line — Lawrie is still the most-capped Hibernian player.

Now a snowy-haired Octogenarian, Lawrie retains his lifelong passion for the Club he graced as a player and is a regular attender at matches, and one of the Club's Champions.

Born in Edinburgh in 1928, Lawrie joined Hibernian in 1945 at the age of 16. He became the final piece in a forward line-up after establishing himself in the team, making his debut in a win against Kilmarnock and then scoring his first goal against Queen of the South.

That line-up was one that was to reverberate around the country — Smith, Johnstone, Reilly, Turnbull and Ormond — as the Famous Five.

But Lawrie's love affair with Hibernian began long before he became one of the Club's greatest-ever players. Brought up near the ground of arch-rivals Hearts, Lawrie never entertained thoughts of supporting the team in maroon. "My family had been Hibs supporters — my dad, my grandad —and we only went to one stadium, Easter Road."

Lifted over the turnstiles, handed a Duncan's hazelnut block as a treat, the young Lawrie learned to love his visits to Easter Road at a time when crowds were huge, and still changed ends at half-time.

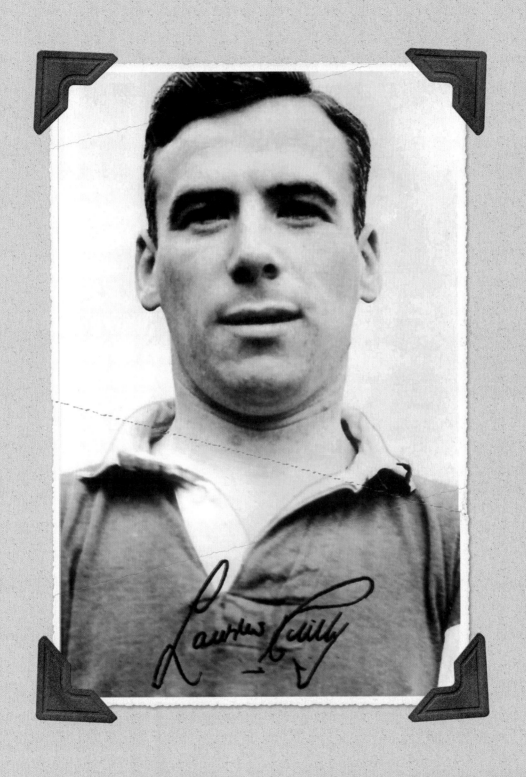

"Last Minute" Lawrie Reilly

"You couldn't teach what Lawrie had.
Those kinds of goalscorers are born, not made."

Lawrie's career at Hibernian ranged from his post-war start until his retirement in 1958. During that glittering period, three league titles were won – in 1947 and then back-to-back in 1950-51 and in 1951-52.

He was part of the Hibernian side that became the first to compete in European Cup football in the inaugural European Cup in 1955. The Famous Five was no longer together, Bobby Johnstone having left for England, but Hibernian were still a force in the game.

Hibs went to German champions Rot-Weiss Essen and thrashed their hosts 4-0. Turnbull, Reilly and Ormond got on the scoresheet, while Smith was denied in the final seconds when the referee blew for full-time before the ball had crossed the line. The sides drew 1-1 in the return match at Easter Road. The side lost to a Raymond Kopa-inspired Reims side in the semi-final.

Lawrie bagged a stunning 232 goals for Hibs during his career. His Famous Five partner Eddie Turnbull said of Lawrie: "You couldn't teach what Lawrie had. Those kinds of goalscorers are born, not made."

But modest as ever, the man himself is keen to ensure team-mates who themselves were no slouches at bulging the net shared in the credit for his exploits, insisting strikers need other players to create chances. "I played with the best. They were out of this world."

Lawrie was also a part of the Hibernian team that thrashed Matt Busby's vaunted Manchester United 7-3 in front of a 70,000-strong testimonial crowd assembled for Gordon Smith in 1952.

He also enjoyed international travel. Quite apart from the early European exploits, Lawrie's Hibernian side were enticed over to Brazil in 1953, playing three times at the Maracana Stadium. The team played to rave reviews in Brazil.

Knee ligament damage, and the emergence of a striking talent named Joe Baker, saw Lawrie retire in 1958. In his final match, against Rangers at Easter Road, the great man did what he did best – netting in a 3-1 win.

Archive Photography: Tom Wright - Old Scotland in Pictures, 107-109 Brunswick Street Edinburgh Midlothian EH7 5HR

LAWRIE
THE SCOTLAND STAR

Lawrie Reilly was inducted into the SFA Hall of Fame in 2005 for his significant contribution to Scottish football.

Still Hibernian's most-capped player, Lawrie's scoring record of 22 goals in 38 appearances in the dark blue means he enjoys a 60 % international strike rate which is greater than that of Kenny Dalglish, Denis Law or Joe Jordan.

In fact, Lawrie stands second only to Hughie Gallacher amongst those capped ten times or more.

He enjoyed a tremendous scoring record against the Auld Enemy, scoring 5 goals in five Wembley appearances. His habit of striking late in these international fixtures was what earned the soubriquet "Last Minute."

His final appearance for the national side came against England in 1957, and was the only time he failed to score at Wembley. One abiding regret Lawrie shares with all Hibernian fans was that the Famous Five never played for Scotland as a complete unit.

1958 Scottish Cup Final Squad v Clyde

Hibs v Rangers 1958

SUMMER SIGNING:

MICHAEL HART

Experience was key to the signing of Michael Hart when the right back joined Hibernian in the summer.

The former Aberdeen and Preston North End star brought huge knowledge gained in the SPL and the Championship – something that Manager John Hughes was keen to land.

Signed on a two-year contract, Michael was described by the manager as "a quality player with lots of experience. We are delighted to be able to add him to our squad and we believe he will make a big contribution here at Hibernian."

Michael's arrival at Easter Road brought to an end a difficult, injury hit two year spell south of the border.

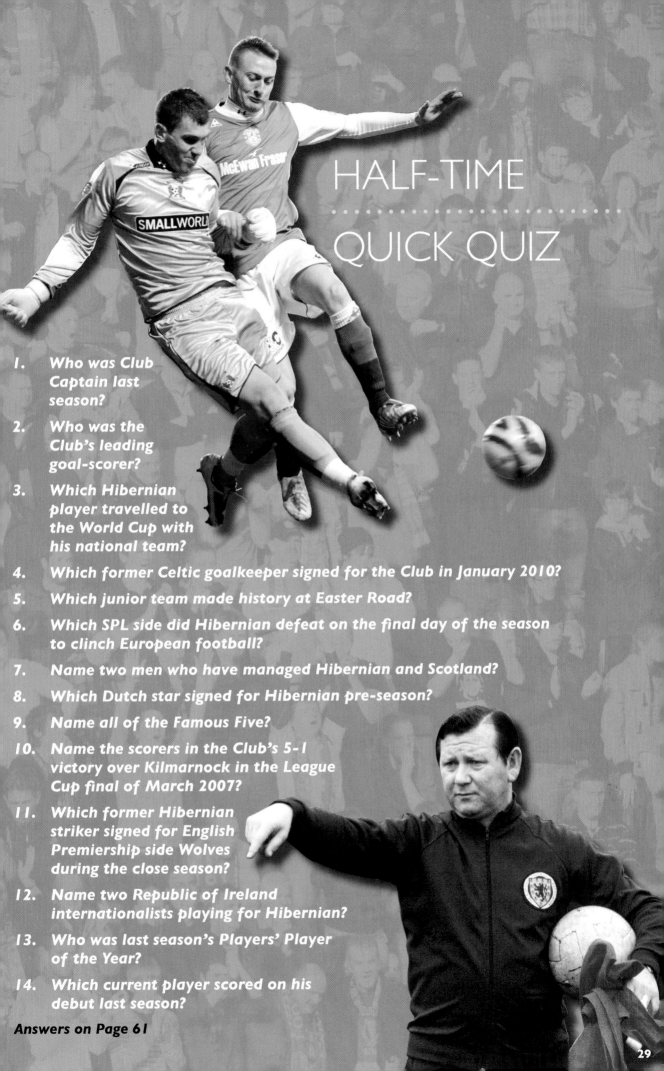

HALF-TIME
QUICK QUIZ

1. Who was Club Captain last season?

2. Who was the Club's leading goal-scorer?

3. Which Hibernian player travelled to the World Cup with his national team?

4. Which former Celtic goalkeeper signed for the Club in January 2010?

5. Which junior team made history at Easter Road?

6. Which SPL side did Hibernian defeat on the final day of the season to clinch European football?

7. Name two men who have managed Hibernian and Scotland?

8. Which Dutch star signed for Hibernian pre-season?

9. Name all of the Famous Five?

10. Name the scorers in the Club's 5-1 victory over Kilmarnock in the League Cup final of March 2007?

11. Which former Hibernian striker signed for English Premiership side Wolves during the close season?

12. Name two Republic of Ireland internationalists playing for Hibernian?

13. Who was last season's Players' Player of the Year?

14. Which current player scored on his debut last season?

Answers on Page 61

29

HIBERNIAN TV

THE INSIDE STORY

Get the inside story direct from Easter Road and get closer to your favourite team by tuning in to the club's online TV channel – Hibernian TV.

Bursting with all the latest news from Easter Road, Hibernian TV takes you behind the scenes and enables you to access the thoughts of both the manager and squad with daily exclusive interviews.

Also make sure you stay on the ball by making Hibernian TV your first port of call for match action – live audio coverage available for all first team matches plus overseas subscribers can watch the drama as it unfolds.

Some of the greatest players to have worn the famous green and white jersey are also regular guests on Hibernian TV; sharing their favourite club memories and discussing their thoughts on the current squad.

The first interview given by our new signings will be aired on Hibernian TV – keeping our viewers one step ahead of the rest of the crowd.

First for the action and post-match reaction, Hibernian TV gives you the opportunity to find out what is happening at YOUR club – available for just 10p per day.

Our match commentary team is packed full of experience, enthusiasm and Hibernian knowledge – bringing you a premium service to your PC and ensuring you share all the glory, goals and drama.

HIBERNIAN BORN & BRED

··

IAN MURRAY

He's the man whose heart is always on his sleeve. Ian Murray's love for Hibernian is never far from view, and his passion for the Club he supports as well as plays for has endeared him to supporters.

Ian Murray

Born: 20th March 1981

Height: 6ft tall

Position: Defender/Midfielder

Previous Clubs: Alloa (loan), Rangers, Norwich City

International Caps: 6

Allied to that is a player with a lion-hearted approach to the game, who never shirks a tackle or draws back from a challenge when he dons the famous green and white.

"Nid" as he is known to team-mates and fans is a local lad and supporter who grew up dreaming of playing for his team, and then did.

So it is no surprise to learn that Ian feels a real sense of pride at the progress of the Club in recent years, with the development of a training centre and the completion of the stadium with the new East Stand.

"Building the training ground was a terrific thing for the club and players and the stadium is the next step. It gives everyone great satisfaction to see the progress made. When I first started out 11 years ago there was not even a stand behind one of the goals."

He is now hoping that he and the rest of the players can build on those foundations and drive success on the field – but he feels there is a real role for supporters.

"The new stand is like a big, steep wall facing the players when they come out of the tunnel. It is great that opposition players and fans compliment us on the ground, but the bottom line is you want it to be an unhappy place for them. When our fans get behind us and we see them there in numbers, making a noise, it lifts the players."

The Club vice-captain takes his role and responsibility seriously. However, there is one new role in his life which involves even more responsibility – as a new father. Ian's baby arrived during the summer.

SUMMER SIGNING:

DAVID STEPHENS

David Stephens provided Hibernian with the Club's biggest signing of the summer – even if the young centre-back was far from a household name.

The Welsh under-19 internationalist stands an imposing 6ft 4ins tall, and he had been tipped for a bright future in the game down south before his decision to head North.

David joined Hibernian on a three-year deal from Norwich City, where he had come through the ranks at that club's renowned Academy.

In clinching his signature, the Club beat off competition from Lincoln City, where David has spent a successful time on loan.

SQUAD PROFILES

Graeme Smith

"Buzz" signed for the Club from Brighton. Terrific reflexes and a willingness to patrol his area marked him out as strong competition for the Number One jersey as he turned in a series of man-of-the-match performances.

Graham Stack

The former Arsenal man provided an assured presence between the posts for much of the season. A top quality shot-stopper, he pulled off several memorable saves. A big personality, his presence in the dressing room assures there is never a dull moment.

Mark Brown

Mark was signed from Celtic, also in the January window, but injury meant he was unable to feature in the team. A proven top keeper at SPL level, he will be hoping to break into the reckoning this season and push on.

Thomas Flynn

From the North East of England, Tom graduated from an all-conquering Hibernian Under-19 side of last season to the first team squad last season. Still developing as a genuine talent.

Sean Welsh

Sean Welsh will be hoping this will be his big breakthrough season. The 20-year-old midfielder skippered the under 19s to an historic treble before signing for the senior squad, only to be hit by a year plagued by injury.

Chris Hogg

"Hoggy" is a big-hearted, no-nonsense centre half who leads by example in his role as Club captain. Chris was signed by Tony Mowbray, but is now one of our longest-serving players having joined Hibernian from Ipswich Town.

Sol Bamba

The 6ft 3in Ivory Coast star turned in several man of the match performances in defence last season, and earned a trip to the African Cup of Nations and the World Cup with his national team. Tall, strong and athletic, Sol has relished the physical battle of Scottish football as well as showing he has excellent ball skills.

Lee Currie

Another graduate of the treble-winning Under 19 side, Lee will be hoping this is his year to make big strides forward. A defender, Lee has benefited from a period out on loan.

Paul Hanlon

Paul can play at full-back or centre-half and played in both positions with great success last season. However, it was at centre-back that he really caught the eye, deputising with great aplomb for Bamba when the big man was on international duty. Tipped for great things.

Steven Thicot

Steven came into his own towards the end of last season, with several strong performances when he finally broke into the starting 11. A product of the famed French Academy system, and an Under 19 internationalist, he is an accomplished defensive player.

Lewis Stevenson

Another product of Hibernian's youth system, Lewis is perhaps unfortunate in that he can play across a number of positions. The utility tag means the young Fifer has struggled to hold down a starting slot, but he is a valued member of the squad who will be hoping to kick on this season.

John Rankin

Pocket sized but big in heart, Rankin is one of the hardest-working players at the Club. The little midfielder gets through a power of work in every game, and his efforts – while often unrecognised by others – are much appreciated by his team-mates.

Merouane Zemmama

The Moroccan wizard is a player who can win matches. Searing pace, trickery on the ball, a strong shot with either foot, his is a rare talent. Injury disrupted his season last year, when he appeared to be rediscovering his best form with some strong performances. Will be hoping for a big year.

Daniel Galbraith

A young man who will undoubtedly be hoping to break into a more regular starting berth this season, Danny is a left-sided winger/midfielder with the ability to beat defenders. He also poses a goal threat, as he showed last season when slotting a last-gasp winner against Celtic at Parkhead.

Kevin McBride

Kevin is an excellent reader of the game, and his strength in protecting the back four and linking play from the back made him an integral part of the team last season. His partnership with Liam Miller forged much of the successful start to last season.

David
Wotherspoon

The Club's Young Player of the Year, David enjoyed an outstanding debut season in the first team after graduating from the Under 19s, kicked off with a goal on his debut against St Mirren at Easter Road. And all of this despite playing much of the season at full-back, rather than in his preferred attacking midfield berth.

Liam Miller

The influential midfielder enjoyed a strong first season at the Club following his move to Edinburgh. The Republic of Ireland international was the Players' Player of the Year after a string of dominant performances when he pulled the strings from the centre of the park.

Colin Nish

Another lifetime Hibs fan, "Big Nishy" played a prominent role last season, in particular in the run-in when he scored five vital goals in two matches to earn the four points which clinched European football. Tall and awkwad, he provides defenders with a stern test.

Derek Riordan

A goalscoring talisman, Derek played an attacking midfield role last season, but even so managed to chip in with plenty of goals from his position wide left.

This return to goal-scoring form, plus an appetite for more workmanlike chores, saw Hibs-daft Derek recalled to the full national set-up.

Anthony Stokes

A goal-scoring machine, the Irish internationalist came second in the SPL charts behind Kris Boyd last season, topping 20 goals. A ruthless finisher, his willingness to take any opportunity saw him score the goal of the season against Ranges at Ibrox. Will be looking to force his way into the Republic's starting 11 this season by playing well week in and week out.

Ian Murray

Athleticism, ball-winning ability, absolute commitment and a winning mentality characterise his approach, and a strong season at left-back showed that Ian is also a potent force driving forward. The Vice-Captain is one of the stalwarts of the side.

WEARING THE ARMBAND

CHRIS HOGG

When Chris Hogg took over the armband at the start of last season following the departure of Rob Jones for Championship side Scunthorpe, the central defender was happy to talk of the pride he felt.

Chris Hogg

Born: 21st March 1985 in Middlesbrough

Height: 6ft tall

Position: Defender

Previous Clubs: York City, Ipswich Town, Boston United (loan)

International Caps: Capped by England at Under 15 and Under 19 level, where his team-mates included Wayne Rooney

Captaining a Club like Hibernian was, he said, an honour. And after his first full season wearing the armband, the likeable Englishman doesn't feel any diminishing of that sense of pride.

The man signed by Tony Mowbray from Ipswich thrives on the responsibility of skippering the sides. "It's a job I take very seriously. It is a great honour to be Captain at Hibernian. I've been with the Club for a few years now and I have learned about the great traditions here. I know how important the Club is to the supporters, and that they expect their Captain to be the embodiment of the Club."

Thoughtful and considered in all of his dealings, the skipper is never one to make rash promises or predictions. However, he feels that the Club is going in the right direction and is happy to play a role in that progress. "I've always tried to be a good professional and to lead by example. I have learned about the Club's achievements, and I'd like to think I can help to add to them."

Hoggy, who hails from the north east of England, began his career in midfield before switching to defending, and credits Tony Mowbray – who coached him at Ipswich before signing him for Hibernian – as one of the biggest influences on his career.

His bravery on the pitch has never been in doubt, but his courage in tackling a robber trying to steal his girlfriend's car in 2005 saw him severely injure an arm, delaying his debut for Hibernian by some months. That spirit has seen him play on through injuries on a number of occasions, winning the hearts and minds of Hibernian fans.

ACADEMY
NEWS

No Club in Scotland is better known for producing and developing talented young footballers than Hibernian.

And the opening of the Hibernian Training Centre in 2007 has seen an added focus on the Club's ability to bring young players through to first team level. Supporters of the Club take particular satisfaction from seeing players they have followed as youngsters break through.

Last season was no exception, with a number of players from the treble-winning Under 19 side breaking into the first team squad.

David Wotherspoon, in particular, made a big impact during the season and was named the Hibernian Players' Young Player of the Year and winning lavish praise from manager John Hughes for his contribution at full-back, in midfield and even played as part of the front three.

Academy manager Bill Hendry is the man charged with overseeing the development of the Club's young players, along with coach Alistair Stevenson and his dedicated team of coaching staff.

A key part of ensuring the supply line of talented youngsters is attracting the best young players to come to the Club in the first place, and in this the new Training Centre has a key role to play – alongside the Club's excellent reputation.

Bill said: "The Training Centre has been a major factor in attracting players from other clubs as all visitors to the Hibernian Training Centre for the first time have been struck by the excellence of the facilities on offer.

"Its existence and the reputation for developing youth at Hibernian continues to make signing for Hibernian a welcome prospect."

David
Wotherspoon

TWO TO WATCH

As ever, we seek to focus on two of the players who have come through our Youth Academy and of whom great things are expected.

Those we have seen "graduate" in recent years include David Wotherspoon, Steven Fletcher, Scott Brown, Kevin Thomson, Steven Whittaker, Derek Riordan and Garry O'Connor, to name but a few.

So can we expect big things of the latest batch?

Scott Taggart

Scott Taggart was the Academy's Player of the Year, and broke into the fringes of the first team squad at the end of last season.

The teenage midfielder is a strapping 6ft 1in tall, and can also operate in defence at right-back. He was delighted to be named amongst the substitutes for one or two matches at the end of the season, and said: "Hopefully if I work hard enough I can get a chance at first team level and build from there – like David Wotherspoon has. What David has done has shown what can be achieved."

A native of North Lanarkshire, Scott signed for Hibs in 2006. Bill Hendry said: "Scott is adaptable and has played in several positions – at full-back, centre-back or midfield. One of his main assets is his ability to drive at defences and shoot from long range."

Scott Smith

Scott Smith has been with the Club since signing from Hearts in 2005. He is approaching his 19th birthday, and stands a little under 6ft tall. Again, adaptability has proven an advantage for the young defender, who is comfortable at centre-half or at left-back.

The youngster hails from Edinburgh and has been capped at every age level for Scotland. Bill Hendry said: "He has a real winning mentality and sets a high standard of leadership."

Bill stressed that both players had benefited from the facilities offered at the Training Centre. "This has been instrumental in their continued development – and not only them but all of the others within the Academy."

HIBS HISTORY
AT A GLANCE

Winners 2007

1875
Founded by members of the Catholic Young Men's Society attached to St Patrick's Church in Edinburgh's **"Little Ireland"** – the Cowgate.

The name derives from Latin and means Irishmen.

1950s
Greatest era to date – The Famous Five years which secured league championships and saw Hibernian as the first British Club to compete in the European Cup, losing at the semi-final stage.

1990
Attempted takeover by Hearts owner Wallace Mercer as Hibernian faces financial melt-down.

1887
Scottish Cup winners, and a defeat of Preston North End the same year saw Hibernian crowned **"World Club Champions"**.

1970s
A second golden era when **"Turnbull's Tornadoes"** won silverware and played thrilling football.

HONOURS:

Scottish League Winners (4) 1902/03, 1947/48, 1950/51, 1951/52

First Division winners (2) 1980/81, 1998/99

Division Two winners (3) 1893/94, 1894/95, 1932/33

Division One runners-up (6) 1896/97, 1946/47, 1949/50, 1952/53, 1973/74, 1974/75

Scottish Cup winners (2) 1887, 1902

Scottish Cup runners-up (9) 1896, 1914, 1923, 1924, 1947, 1958, 1972, 1979, 2001

Scottish League Cup winners (3) 1972/73, 1991/92, 2006/07

Scottish League Cup runners-up (6) 1950/51, 1968/69, 1974/75, 1985/86, 1993/94, 2003/04

Drybrough Cup winners (2) 1972/73, 1973/74

Summer Cup winners (2) 1941, 1964

1990s
Stadium redeveloped at the turn of the decade.

2007
Club opens Hibernian Training Centre in December.

1991
Present owner Sir Tom Farmer CBE saves the Club from extinction, and a League Cup win follows shortly after.

2007
Hibernian wins League Cup in 5-1 win over Kilmarnock.

2010
Stadium redevelopment completed with the opening of new East Stand during the summer.

EASTER ROAD STADIUM

NEW EAST STAND

The redevelopment of Easter Road Stadium was completed in the summer of 2010 with the new East Stand, giving the ground a capacity of more than 20,000 and confirming the stadium as the finest in Scotland outside of Glasgow.

Manager John Hughes helping to launch Lothian Hibernian – Hibernian Community Foundation Partnership

WINNING PRAISE

· · · · · · · · · · · · · · · · · ·

WITHIN THE COMMUNITY

The prestigious Annual Clydesdale Bank Premier League Awards threw up two winners for Hibernian.

Anthony Stokes' stunning goal against Rangers at Ibrox ran away with the award as the league's goal of the season.

But a less high profile success was equally important for a Club that prides itself on being rooted in its community.

The award of Best Community Initiative is always fiercely contested, as the Clubs seek to demonstrate their commitment to their local communities.

However it was Hibernian who came out on top for the Under 19s Community Engagement Initiative. Working with Hibernian Community Foundation, the Club trained the under 19 players as SFA coaches and referees.

The youngsters are then involved in coaching and refereeing matches and training sessions for local primary school children and - notably - Lothian Hibernian.

Lothian Hibernian is a unique partnership between Hibernian Community Foundation and Lothian Special Olympics, and has created positive opportunities for players within the sport of learning disability football across the Lothians.

Bill Hendry, Academy Manager being presented with the Best Community Initiative

HIBERNIAN LEARNING CENTRE

The Community Foundation works "to harness the power and passion of football to promote learning, improve health and enhance opportunities within our communities."

As well as the Lothian Hibernian initiative, the Hibernian Learning Centre has been developed and is housed in the South Stand. In partnership with Jewel & Esk College, the Learning Centre has delivered tens of thousands of learning hours for a wide range of people - many of whom might not otherwise be engaged in the education and learning process.

Those taking part are engaged in learning a range of new skills, including IT, numeracy and literacy, and multimedia and the courses all involve recognised qualifications.

Educational tours have also been developed, and again these provide dynamic multi-learning experiences that young people can really enjoy whilst delivering clear educational outcomes under Curriculum for Excellence.

Hibernian Chief Executive Scott Lindsay, who is also a Director of the Foundation, said: "All involved with Lothian Hibernian deserve great credit - those who play for the side first and foremost, but also those people who work to support them in many capacities, including coaching.

"Whilst Lothian Special Olympics has been a well run and well established organisation for many years, this is a terrific example of how football play a really positive role in people's lives, and how - working in partnership through the Foundation - the power of the Club can be harnessed."

HIBERNIAN COMMUNITY FOUNDATION

learning, health & opportunity

SCOTTISH CHARITY NO: SC039699

For those interested in learning more about the work of the foundation, information is available via the Club website, **www.hibernianfc.co.uk**

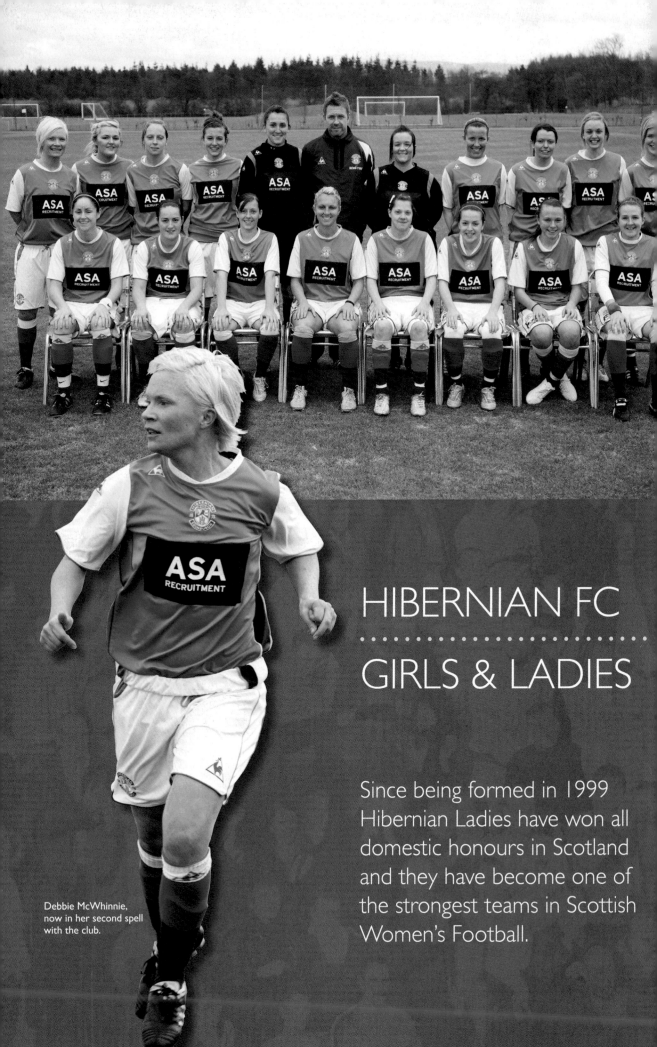

Debbie McWhinnie, now in her second spell with the club.

HIBERNIAN FC

GIRLS & LADIES

Since being formed in 1999 Hibernian Ladies have won all domestic honours in Scotland and they have become one of the strongest teams in Scottish Women's Football.

In that short decade they have won the Scottish Cup FOUR times, League Cup TWICE and the Scottish Women's Premier League THREE times.

With the advent of summer football in 2010, and with a new coaching structure in place, they are hoping to push on to win further honours.

The highlight of the successes enjoyed undoubtedly came in the 2006/2007 season, when Hibernian broke new records in Scotland, going an entire league season without dropping a single point. As well as this they lifted the Scottish Cup in emphatic style with a convincing 5-1 victory over nearest rivals Glasgow City. The Ladies have represented Scotland in the Women's UEFA Cup three times and in 2007 narrowly missed out on qualifying to the next stage of the competition. From 2003 when Hibs Ladies first won major trophies until season 2007-2008, Hibs has been a dominant force in Scottish Women's Football.

In recent years there has been real growth in numbers of girls playing for Hibernian Girls and Ladies FC ,where there are now at least two teams at each age group. The structure now provides a pathway for talented girls to play for a Premier League side and for Scotland.

Teams in 2010 within Hibernian Girls & Ladies are the Ladies A side, Ladies 2000, Ladies 1875, and then the girls at age groups U-17s, U-15s and U-13s.

The squads contain many internationalists at every age level, demonstrating the strength in depth of the organisation.

Hibernian Football Club continues to support Hibernian Girls & Ladies, in particular through the provision of coaching staff and access to facilities at Hibernian Training Centre. All of those involved in recent years deserve great credit.

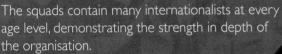

Above: Claire Emslie, a product of the Hibernian Youth Team, in action against Kilmarnock Ladies earlier last season, a game Hibernian won 19-0.

Below: Laura Kennedy and Hollie Thomson warming up for the same game.

HIBS KIDS

The Future Of The Hibernian Family

Hibs Kids membership is open to all Hibee-mad youngsters aged 0-14 years, and is the ideal way to cheer on the team, meet the players and manager and become one of the Hibernian Family.

For just £10 per season Hibs Kids membership includes a Membership Card, discounts for Green Shoots football training courses at the Hibernian Training Centre, 15% discount at the Clubstore on Hibs Kids Days, free access to Hibs Kids match days at Easter Road, a free Christmas Panto, free Easter Holiday Football Festival and a birthday card from the manager along with a new-look newsletter and other super offers.

In addition, you can take out a Hibs Kids Membership for a one-off payment of £50 which lasts until you are 15 years old.

For those wanting to see more of their heroes in action, an Under-15 season ticket is available which offers a fantastic value for money package including access to all SPL matches, priority tickets for European matches and a Clubstore discount voucher redeemeable against our fantastic kit.

CONTACT
DETAILS

General Enquiries

club@hibernianfc.co.uk

Tel: 0131 661 2159

Corporate & Commercial Manager

Russell Smith

rsmith@hibernianfc.co.uk

Tel: 0131 656 7072

Match-day Hospitality & Advertising

Amanda Vettese

Corporate Hospitality Manager

avettese@hibernianfc.co.uk

Tel: 0131 656 7073

New Media Manager

Andrew Sleight

asleight@hibernianfc.co.uk

Tel: 0131 656 7079

Ticket Operations

Judith Ireland

Ticket Office Manager

jireland@hibernianfc.co.uk

Tel: 0844 844 1875 (Option 2)

Communications & Press Manager

Elaine Morrison

emorrison@hibernianfc.co.uk

Tel: 0131 656 7076

Conference & Banqueting

All Enquiries to:

Tel: 0131 656 7075

Retail Manager

Paul McFarlane

pmcfarlane@hibernianfc.co.uk

Tel: 0131 656 7097

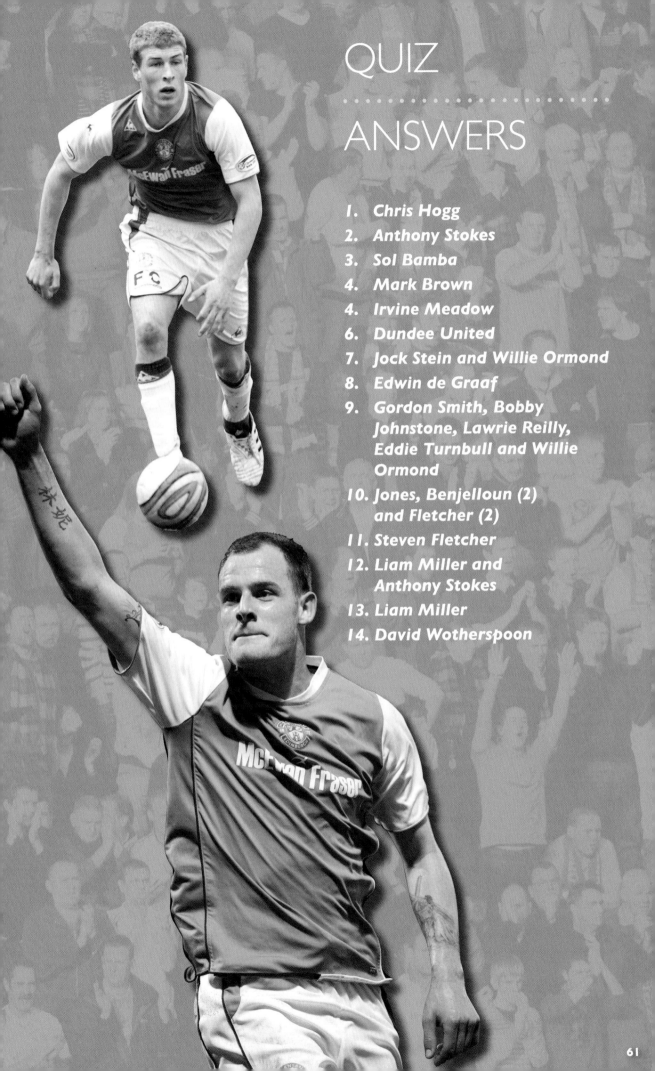

QUIZ
....
ANSWERS

1. **Chris Hogg**
2. **Anthony Stokes**
3. **Sol Bamba**
4. **Mark Brown**
4. **Irvine Meadow**
6. **Dundee United**
7. **Jock Stein and Willie Ormond**
8. **Edwin de Graaf**
9. **Gordon Smith, Bobby Johnstone, Lawrie Reilly, Eddie Turnbull and Willie Ormond**
10. **Jones, Benjelloun (2) and Fletcher (2)**
11. **Steven Fletcher**
12. **Liam Miller and Anthony Stokes**
13. **Liam Miller**
14. **David Wotherspoon**